SURVIVE IN THE MOUNTAINS WITH THE U.S. RANGERS AND ARMY MOUNTAIN DIVISION

ELITE FORCES SURVIVAL GUIDE SERIES

Elite Survival
Survive in the Desert with the French Foreign Legion
Survive in the Arctic with the Royal Marine Commandos
Survive in the Mountains with the U.S. Rangers and Army
  Mountain Division
Survive in the Jungle with the Special Forces "Green Berets"
Survive in the Wilderness with the Canadian and Australian
  Special Forces
Survive at Sea with the U.S. Navy SEALs
Training to Fight with the Parachute Regiment
The World's Best Soldiers

Elite Operations and Training
Escape and Evasion
Surviving Captivity with the U.S. Air Force
Hostage Rescue with the SAS
How to Pass Elite Forces Selection
Learning Mental Endurance with the U.S. Marines

Special Forces Survival Guidebooks
Survival Equipment
Navigation and Signaling
Surviving Natural Disasters
Using Ropes and Knots
Survival First Aid
Trapping, Fishing, and Plant Food
Urban Survival Techniques

SURVIVE IN THE MOUNTAINS WITH THE U.S. RANGERS AND ARMY MOUNTAIN DIVISION

CHRIS McNAB

**Introduction by Colonel John T. Carney. Jr., USAF–Ret.
President, Special Operations Warrior Foundation**

MASON CREST PUBLISHERS

This edition first published in 2003
by Mason Crest Publishers Inc.
370 Reed Road, Broomall, PA, 19008

Library of Congress Cataloging-in-Publication Data available

ISBN 1-59084-003-8

Editorial and design by
Amber Books Ltd.
Bradley's Close
74–77 White Lion Street
London N1 9PF

Project Editor Chris Stone
Designer Simon Thompson
Picture Research Lisa Wren

Printed and bound in Malaysia

10 9 8 7 6 5 4 3 2 1

ACKNOWLEDGMENT

For authenticating this book, the Publishers would like to thank the Public Affairs Offices of the U.S. Special Operations Command, MacDill AFB, FL.; Army Special Operations Command, Fort Bragg, N.C.; Navy Special Warfare Command, Coronado, CA.; and the Air Force Special Operations Command, Hurlbert Field, FL.

IMPORTANT NOTICE
The survival techniques and information described in this publication are for use in dire circumstances where the safety of the individual is at risk. Accordingly, the publisher cannot accept any responsibility for any prosecution or proceedings brought or instituted against any person or body as a result of the uses or misuses of the techniques and information within.

DEDICATION
This book is dedicated to those who perished in the terrorist attacks of September 11, 2001, and to the Special Forces soldiers who continually serve to defend freedom.

Picture Credits
Corbis: 12, 20, 24, 26, 28, 35, 36, 52, 54, 55, 56, 58, 63, 66, 72, 80, 89; **Military Picture Library:** 30/31; **TRH:** 6, 8, 17, 25, 32, 34, 42, 48, 60, 65, 69, 70, 73, 75, 77, 79, 85; **US Dept. of Defence:** 19
Illustrations courtesy of De Agostini UK and the following supplied by Patrick Mulrey: 39, 51, 53, 82, 83
Front cover: **Corbis** (both)

CONTENTS

INTRODUCTION

Elite forces are the tip of Freedom's spear. These small, special units are universally the first to engage, whether on reconnaissance missions into denied territory for larger, conventional forces or in direct action, surgical operations, preemptive strikes, retaliatory action, and hostage rescues. They lead the way in today's war on terrorism, the war on drugs, the war on transnational unrest, and in humanitarian operations as well as nation building. When large scale warfare erupts, they offer theater commanders a wide variety of unique, unconventional options.

Most such units are regionally oriented, acclimated to the culture and conversant in the languages of the areas where they operate. Since they deploy to those areas regularly, often for combined training exercises with indigenous forces, these elite units also serve as peacetime "global scouts" and "diplomacy multipliers," a beacon of hope for the democratic aspirations of oppressed peoples all over the globe.

Elite forces are truly "quiet professionals": their actions speak louder than words. They are self-motivated, self-confident, versatile, seasoned, mature individuals who rely on teamwork more than daring-do. Unfortunately, theirs is dangerous work. Since "Desert One"—the 1980 attempt to rescue hostages from the U.S. embassy in Tehran, for instance—American special operations forces have suffered casualties in real world operations at close to fifteen times the rate of U.S. conventional forces. By the very nature of the challenges which face special operations forces, training for these elite units has proven even more hazardous.

Thus it's with special pride that I join you in saluting the brave men and women who volunteer to serve in and support these magnificent units and who face such difficult challenges ahead.

Colonel John T. Carney, Jr., USAF–Ret.
President, Special Operations Warrior Foundation

To become an elite U.S. Army mountain soldier is not easy. In the U.S. Rangers alone, about 50 percent of recruits fail during training.

A HISTORY OF MOUNTAIN SOLDIERS

Make a mistake on a mountain, and it will not forgive you. Mountains are dangerous places in which to survive and fight. That is why armies have specialized mountain-warfare units. Two of the best are the U.S. Rangers and the 10th Mountain Division.

Since it was first formed in 1775, the U.S. Army has served with distinction in wars all around the world. Because it can be called to serve anywhere, its soldiers have become experts in outdoor survival, including mountain operations.

Looking back into history, the U.S. Army began as a force called the Continental Army in the late eighteenth century. The United States at that time was facing the turmoil of revolution. The British rulers had placed harsh laws upon the American colonies, and a group of American leaders gathered to work out how they would achieve independence.

On June 14, 1775, at a meeting called the Second Continental Congress, the Continental Army was formed under the command of **George Washington**. It was this army that fought to expel the British during the **Revolutionary War** between 1775 and 1783. The Continental Army was originally only 960 men strong. Yet it was to be the seed from which the U.S. Army would grow.

A U.S. Ranger abseils down a cliff. The name "Rangers" comes from a band of U.S. troops who fought Native Americans in the 1700s.

Following the war, the Continental Army was disbanded. Now that independence was achieved, it was replaced by the U.S. Army. The president was the power behind the Army—he still is today. As commander-in-chief, the president could order the Army into battle whenever he felt it was right. But the country could not afford to keep a huge army all the time during its early days. That is why the U.S. Army grew or shrunk in size depending on whether or not the country was at war. Major wars over the next century made sure the U.S. Army became combat-tested. In 1812, the Army was once again fighting the British, in what was called the War of 1812. Between 1846 and 1848 U.S. soldiers were fighting in Mexico. But the biggest leap for the U.S. Army happened between 1861 and 1865 during the **American**

This officer of the 10th Mountain Division in World War II carries the standard issue M1 Garand rifle.

Civil War. Remarkably, the U.S. Army expanded over the four years of civil war to a massive force of around one million men.

Over the next 50 years, the U.S. Army went through many changes in size and organization. In 1917, it entered World War I. Europe had been locked in bloody battle for nearly three years, and Britain, France, and their allies were almost exhausted. The United States arrived in battle as one of the best trained and prepared armies in the world at that time. It had over three and a half million men at arms, and some of the most advanced equipment available. The fighting was hard and the United States lost thousands of men, but by 1918 the war ended with Germany defeated.

Yet the biggest test of all for the U.S. Army came in 1941. World War II had been raging across Europe since 1939, but in 1941 the Japanese bombed the U.S. fleet at **Pearl Harbor**. The United States was now in the war. Millions of men across the United States were called up to serve in the Army and it grew to over eight million men. These men served right across the globe— the Far East, Africa, and Europe. They fought huge battles with German and Japanese forces. Tough and experienced German units were amazed at how quickly U.S. recruits became hard fighting soldiers, and the U.S. contribution to the war meant that victory for the Allies was certain. Both Germany and Japan surrendered in 1945. During World War II, the U.S. Army was also reorganized into different parts—each part called a Command. There were Army Ground Forces, Army Air Forces (the Air Force would become separate in 1947), and Army Service Forces. The Women's Army Corps was also formed in 1942.

World War II showed what a remarkable fighting force the U.S. Army had become. Since 1945, it has continued to prove this in many conflicts around the world. Wars in Korea, Vietnam, and the Middle East have proved that the U.S. Army can operate in all terrains and environments. This includes mountains.

It was basically during World War II that armies around the world recognized the need for elite mountain units. World War II saw fighting in almost every environment, from the deserts of North Africa to the icy wastes of Russia. Mountains also became battlegrounds. Mountains are important places for armies to train in because their height means that they can command a large area around them, and they are difficult to take by attacking armies.

The Mountain Training Center for the 10th Mountain Division was first established on September 3, 1942, at Camp Carson, Colorado. Its initial goal was to find new ways of mountain-fighting.

GRENADA

During the rescue mission conducted in Grenada in 1983, the Rangers did a daring parachute jump from only 500 feet (152 m) onto the Point Salines airfield. As soon as they landed, they were into action and captured the airfield after overcoming all resistance.

Difficult, but not impossible, as the world's elite mountain units have shown.

The U.S. Army developed training schools in mountain warfare back in the 1940s, in particular the Mountain Training Center at Camp Carson in Colorado. Special mountain units were created, such as the 87th Mountain Infantry Battalion. Today, the Army has its own Mountain Warfare School. This takes regular soldiers and trains them in all the special techniques of mountain survival and combat. This includes climbing, navigating, survival skills, and hunting. Only soldiers who are incredibly fit can complete the course, but those that complete it are mountain experts.

The United States was one of the pioneers in forming mountain units. Two units in particular have become famous in this role—the U.S. Army Rangers and the 10th Mountain Division. The 10th Light Division (Alpine) was formed in July 1943. The U.S. Army had entered World War II in December 1941, and it knew it might have to fight in mountainous environments in Italy and northern Europe. So it set to work training elite mountain forces, pushing the men through tough exercises on some of the highest peaks in the United States. The result was men who could survive in the harshest mountain conditions, and who were excellent climbers and skiers.

In 1944 the unit was renamed 10th Mountain Division.

They were also tough fighters, as they would prove when they went to war in the Italian mountains in 1945.

During the fighting there, they took German mountain positions that the Germans thought were impregnable, including climbing the 1,500 feet (456 m) up the vertical face of a cliff to attack enemy positions at the top. They lost many men during these battles, but they showed that even the tallest mountains could be taken by the 10th.

The 10th performed courageously throughout the war. When the war finished,

A Rangers Sergeant goes into action on Grenada in 1983. He had just landed after parachuting from 500 feet (152 m).

many of the 10th went on to start ski schools and survival groups. Yet changes in the Army structure meant that the 10th Mountain Division became the 10th Infantry Division in 1954, but even this was then disbanded in 1958. However, mountain warfare specialists are something every army needs. So on 13 February 1985, the 10th Mountain Division was reformed. Since then it has regained its reputation as mountain warfare specialists, training its men in advanced climbing, survival, and combat techniques. The Division has fought all over the world, not just on mountains, in places including the deserts of the Middle East during the Gulf War, and during the amphibious operations against Haiti in 1994. Yet mountain warfare remains its specialty, and it adds an essential element to the strength of the U.S. armed forces. As recently as September 2001 it was placed on high alert following the terrorist attacks on America.

The badge of the 10th Mountain Division, featuring crossed swords.

Another U.S. Army unit best known for its mountain survival and warfare talents is the U.S. Rangers. The Rangers were formed in 1942 as an elite unit to fight the Germans during the Second World War. The officer chosen to lead the "new" Rangers was Major William Darby. He took his recruits from all branches of the

U.S. Army. The lucky 500 who survived the two-week selection course of speed marches and assault courses, went on to further training as the elite First Ranger Battalion. (The Rangers were to establish a U.S. Army record by doing a 15-mile (24-km) speed march in two hours.)

At the **Achnacarry Commando School** in Scotland, the Rangers underwent more intensive training. This included lessons in the art of mountain survival. In April 1943, the 2nd Ranger Battalion, formed in the United States, was sent to Britain for training in cliff assault techniques, to be used on the coastline of Normandy on **D-Day** (June 6, 1944)—the Allied invasion of German-occupied France. When the Rangers went ashore, they faced some of the toughest opposition in their short history. The Rangers were given just 30 minutes to destroy a battery of 155-millimeter guns before the first wave of infantry landed. Rocket-fired grappling hooks were to be used to scale the steep cliff face. Yet the top of the cliffs was heavily defended. More than half of the Rangers were dead or injured before the top was reached. On the top, they found a single artillery piece, which had already been destroyed by naval gun fire. Though

WEAPONS

A Ranger squad is heavily armed. Each man has an M16 rifle, and other squad weapons include machine guns, grenade launchers, and explosives. Combine this firepower with their training and they are a formidable force.

this was a bitter disappointment, the Rangers would have success in fighting the Germans throughout Europe. General Norman Cota gave a now immortal command, "Rangers, lead the way."

When World War II ended, the Rangers were almost straight back into battle in the mountainous country of Korea. Communist North Korea had invaded South Korea, and the U.S. Army and many other Allied armies went into action to stop the South falling to the communists. The **Ranger Training Center** (Airborne) at Fort Benning, Georgia, was created to train the first companies. By January 1951, eight companies had completed the four-week cold-weather course at Camp Carson. This taught them how to stay alive in hostile mountainous climates, such as those in Korea.

U.S. Mountain troops during surveillance training in Norway. Waiting and watching for hours is particularly demanding in mountain climates, where temperatures can reach a low of –72°F (–50°C).

The Rangers were used for some of the toughest assignments of the Korean War. They sometimes parachuted deep behind enemy lines to capture vital towns, or were thrown into battle to hold "lost" positions or spearhead counterattacks. They also conducted reconnaissance patrols, raids, and ambushes as befitting elite infantry. As the fighting in Korea ended, the Rangers were again deactivated. Only the Ranger School at Fort Benning remained. The Ranger School went on to be the place where many of the U.S. Army's elite troops were trained, including the famous U.S. Special Forces.

Ranger School tested a man's endurance, aggression and confidence. It produced men who could survive the most arduous and dangerous conditions. The Ranger was expected to be ready to fight in the jungles, mountains, or icy wastes of the tundra as regular infantry, or in small groups behind enemy lines. He was trained in cliff assaults, survival, climbing, unarmed combat, demolitions, and escape. Many of these men were sent deep into the mountainous jungles of Vietnam during the **Vietnam War**. Since Vietnam, the Rangers have served on combat missions in Panama, Grenada, the Gulf War, and Somalia. On every mission they have proved to be tough warriors, and they have added to the respect the U.S. Army holds across the world.

The badge of Second Ranger Airborne Battalion. This battalion rescued U.S. citizens on Grenada in 1983.

Mountain soldiers are often called out in emergencies. Here, soldiers of the 10th Mountain Division help to clear tons of snow and ice in the village of Copenhagen, New York, in 1998.

The Rangers have fought in almost every environment imaginable. Since the days of World War II, they have been some of the world's greatest mountain warfare specialists. From the snowy mountainsides of Italy in World War II to the highlands of Korea and Vietnam, the Rangers have an intimate knowledge of what it takes to survive at inhospitable altitudes and still remain alert and strong. Ranger training includes a full mountaineering course on some of the toughest peaks in the United States.

The Rangers and 10th Mountain Division have some of the best mountain survival experts anywhere. Whether climbing up a sheer rock face or surviving an **avalanche**, they can teach us how to survive in the incredibly hostile environments found on mountains.

MOUNTAINOUS TERRAIN AND CLIMATE

Mountains offer little protection from low temperatures and high winds. The U.S. Army understands the dangers of the mountain environment better than most other soldiers in the world.

Mountains are dangerous places in which to try and survive. Mountains usually exist in ranges, which consist of peaks, ridges, and valleys between the mountains. Although some mountains stand on their own, mountains are usually formed in a group. These groups of mountains form a long system of mountain ridges, linking one mountain to the next. Closely connected ridges are called mountain systems, and more than one system joined together is called a mountain chain. A mixture of ranges, systems, and chains is called a belt or cordillera.

The climate you might experience on a mountain varies from place to place. However, there is one guiding rule—the higher you go, the colder it gets. Temperature falls at a more or less constant rate with increasing altitude—about 33 to 34°F (0.5–1°C) for every 328 feet (110 m). Wind systems are forced by mountains to rise, and they cool as they do so, causing high rain or snowfall on the slopes that face into the wind. When the wind descends down the sheltered slope, it warms up and the rainfall reduces. Not all

In ancient times, mountains were regarded as holy places. The Meru mountain of India was seen as a place where heaven and earth met.

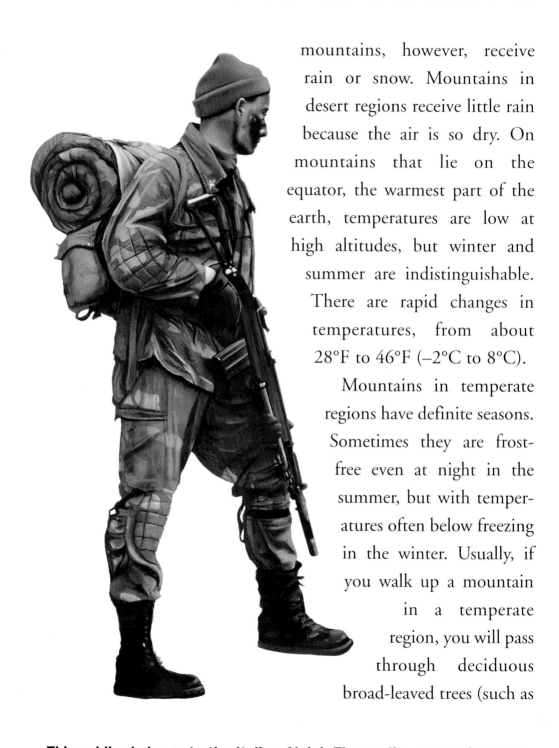

mountains, however, receive rain or snow. Mountains in desert regions receive little rain because the air is so dry. On mountains that lie on the equator, the warmest part of the earth, temperatures are low at high altitudes, but winter and summer are indistinguishable. There are rapid changes in temperatures, from about 28°F to 46°F (–2°C to 8°C).

Mountains in temperate regions have definite seasons. Sometimes they are frost-free even at night in the summer, but with temperatures often below freezing in the winter. Usually, if you walk up a mountain in a temperate region, you will pass through deciduous broad-leaved trees (such as

This soldier belongs to the Italian Alpini. These elite mountain troops often wear a black eagle feather in their hat to distinguish themselves.

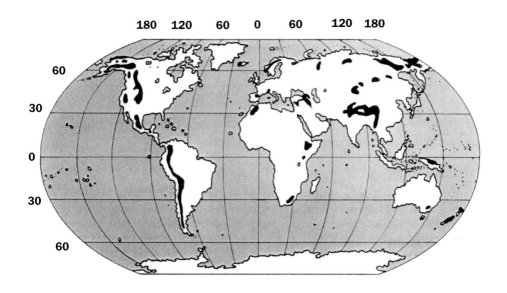

The shaded areas above show the world's largest mountain ranges. The Rocky Mountains range from New Mexico to British Columbia.

oak and sycamore), then evergreen coniferous forest (pine trees). Then you reach what is called the **timberline**—the area where few trees grow at all because of the high altitude. After this, there is an area of tundra-like shrubs and herbs. After that, vegetation can be almost nonexistent.

Whatever the weather you expect, every soldier knows that mountain weather is an unpredictable thing, and they treat it with great respect. Storms can descend in seconds. Flash floods can bring tons of mud flowing down the mountainside, snapping trees like matchsticks. Temperatures can go from warm to freezing in only a few hours. But the weather is only one of the problems the elite soldier faces in training.

CREVASSES

Crevasses are one of the greatest hazards of ice-covered mountains. Some of them are so deep that people have fallen down them and never been seen again despite many rescue attempts.

Mountains are hostile and dangerous. Freezing winds, driving snow, ice fields, mist, rain, and sheer drops of hundreds of feet (many tens of meters) are all potential killers. The soldier must learn how to negotiate them all to reach civilization. In normal circum-

A soldier stands in freezing mountain conditions in southern Russia. Temperatures in Russia can dip as low as –58°F (–50°C) in some remote parts, so layers of warm clothing are essential.

U.S. mountain troops watch out for crevasses, which can be up to 65 feet (20 m) wide, 148 feet (45 m) deep, and hundreds of feet long.

stances, mountains and ice fields should be climbed only by experienced and properly equipped mountaineer troops. However, if you are stranded in mountainous terrain, you must know how to get yourself out of danger and back to civilization. The U.S. Army can tell you all that you need to know about mountain terrain.

On mountains, you are likely to encounter snow, ice, and winds, and may come into close contact with **crevasses** and avalanches of earth, rock, and snow. Mountains have many different types of surfaces. Some have hard, bare rock, which can be either jagged (which is better for climbing because it provides lots of handholds and footholds) or worn smooth and slippery by the weather over thousands of years. Another especially dangerous surface is that of loose small stones on a steep slope. On this surface, there is the danger that you can slip and start to slide down the mountain, gathering speed. Once you get going, it is hard to stop.

The most prominent feature of mountains is the steepness of their **gradient** (the angle at which they go up). This can vary from a gentle slope that is easy to walk on, to walls of ice or rock that go straight up at a vertical angle or can even lean out over the climber's head. Whatever the case, troops will not attempt to climb a

A wounded man is hoisted out of a deep crevasse in the Glacier National Park, MT. The part includes more than 2,000 square miles (3,200 sq km) of the Rocky Mountains in its territory.

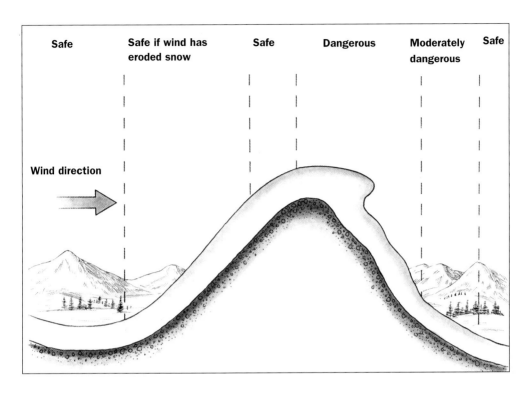

| Safe | Safe if wind has eroded snow | Safe | Dangerous | Moderately dangerous | Safe |

Wind direction

This diagram shows the most dangerous zones for avalanches. In the United States, potential avalanches are watched by the Forest Service of the U.S. Department of Agriculture.

mountain without full professional climbing training. Even then, they must have the good sense not to attempt mountains that are too dangerous.

A special, and very dangerous, feature of mountains is the **glacier**. Glaciers are slow-moving masses of ice. Glacial streams can run just under the surface of the snow or ice, creating weak spots, or they may run on the surface and cause slick, very slippery ice. A glacier is basically a river of ice that flows at a speed that depends largely on its size and the slope on which it travels. It has two parts: the lower glacier and the upper glacier. The lower glacier has an ice surface without snow during the summer. The upper glacier is covered with layers of snow that turns into glacier ice.

There are several features that all elite troops should know if they are forced to travel across them.

Glacial ice

Ice is smooth near the surface of a glacier, but not smooth enough to prevent cracking as it moves. These cracks in the glacier surface are called crevasses.

Ice fall

Ice fall happens where a glacier goes up a steep slope. At the point where the angle goes steeper, there are massive ice blocks, troughs, and crevasses.

Glaciers are massive moving ice sheets. Parts of the Columbia Glacier in Alaska move between 16 and 83 feet (5–25 m) each day.

Glacial rivers

These vary in type. They can present problems if you have to cross them. Melting snow results in large quantities of water pouring down the mountainside. The sun's heat can release huge quantities of water from glaciers, resulting in many rivers and reservoirs forming under an ice surface. These can make the ice surface unstable to walk on.

Flooding glaciers

These are glaciers from which torrents of water flow. They are caused by the violent release of water that the glacier has carried or which the glacier has dammed up as it travels. The water is released by a crevasse or a break in the moving glacial dam.

Moraines

The glacier picks up crushed rock, which is known as **moraine**. The rock may then be deposited in ridges along the side (lateral moraine),

SHELTER

The winds on top of a high mountain can easily reach hurricane force. Tents, equipment, and people can be thrown off the mountain in these conditions, so the soldier needs to find a solid shelter. At such high altitudes and on steep slopes, trees find it hard to grow, so finding wood with which to build your shelter can be scarce. Any material you do use, you will probably have to take with you.

along the center (medial moraine), and at the end of the glacier (terminal moraine). Moraines can be loose and dangerous to cross.

Crevasses

Crevasses are found where a glacier starts at a valley wall, changes direction, or spreads out in a winding valley. They vary in width from a few inches (several centimeters) to hundreds of yards (meters). They can be covered with a thin layer of snow and are thus rendered invisible—until you suddenly fall through them.

From this list of features, it is obvious that soldiers in the mountains must keep very alert to the dangers that surround them. One of the most important points in the training of U.S. Army soldiers is teaching them how to move safely, and that is what they will teach us in the next chapter.

U.S. mountain troops run across a stretch of the Rocky Mountains during a survival exercise in Montana. Enemy troops are not their only concern. They must watch for crevasses and ice falls.

MOVING IN THE MOUNTAINS

A mountain top is an exposed and dangerous place. That is why the U.S. Army's first lesson for the survivor is to get lower down the mountain as quickly and safely as possible.

On a mountain, if you are not going to be rescued quickly, you must get down into the valleys, toward civilization and away from the cold and wet. Do not move in conditions where you cannot see properly or at night—you could injure yourself. Take time to look at the entire area around you. Look for a valley—it will probably be the beginning of a small stream or river. Select a safe route to get to it and find a way down.

When traveling downhill, the elite troops watch out for the following points. Do not go into avalanche chutes. These are places down which you think an avalanche might happen—remember, you cannot outrun an avalanche. If you are on a high ridge, do not walk on rock or snow that hangs over the drop—they may break off under your weight. Try not to travel in thigh- or waist-deep snow—you will find it physically exhausting. South- and west-facing slopes offer hard surfaces late in the day after the surface has been exposed to the sun and then been refrozen. East- and north-facing slopes are generally soft and unstable. Slopes

A soldier uses an ice axe to climb an icy ridge. Some axes are so strong that they can take over 7,000 pounds (2,600 kg) of breaking strain.

Navigating snowy terrain by walking in single file has two key advantages. It is easier to ski in someone's tracks than over fresh snow, and the person in front of you can shield you from the wind.

darkened by rocks or uprooted trees and vegetation provide more footing. Travel in the early morning after a cold night—snow conditions will be more stable then. Try to travel in shaded areas—the sun can make snow unstable.

If there are a number of you (like on a Ranger patrol), travel in single file. Try to walk around crevasses because it is generally much easier to do this than to try to force a crossing. A snow bridge over a crevasse must be carefully examined. If snow covers the bridge, the person at the front must probe the immediate area closely to see if it is strong enough to take your weight. Be prepared for a sudden drop.

If the bridge is narrow or weak, a team can cross it by slithering on their stomachs. This spreads the weight of the human body

Rope bridges are difficult to negotiate. Some rope bridges in Africa stretch an incredible 387 feet (118 m) across deep mountain ravines.

Mountain warfare clothing must give total protection from the elements. Military-issue mountain clothing gives protection from temperatures as low as −70°F (−57°C).

AVALANCHES

Avalanches are truly lethal. They can throw tons of snow down a mountainside at over 100 miles per hour (160 km/h). Getting buried under all this snow can be like getting buried in concrete—it is often impossible to move. Death will occur if you are not found very quickly.

over a broader area. If you feel the bridge is not safe but it is the only route available, send across the lightest person first. (Ensure he or she is securely tied to other members of the party.) Everyone should then follow, walking with light steps and taking care to step exactly in the same tracks.

Bridges vary in strength according to the temperature. In the cold of winter or early morning, the thinnest and most fragile of bridges may have a very high strength. However, when the ice crystals melt in the warmer afternoon temperature, even the most sturdy looking bridge may suddenly collapse.

If you decide to jump over a crevasse, you must follow these points of advice from the U.S. Army.

- Decide whether you are going to make a standing jump or a running jump.
- Pack the snow down if you are planning a running jump.
- Locate the precise edge of the crevasse before jumping.
- Remove all bulky clothing and equipment before you jump.

Approach a crevasse at right angles and, if jumping one, remember that snow may be loose on the far side. Make sure you fall forward after the jump, preferably with an **ice axe** to dig in at the other side. Keep an eye out for anything unusual in the surface of the snow, such as dark patches or dips, which may be covering another crevasse.

When traveling *up* a snow slope, **traversing** (zigzagging) is much easier than going straight up. In soft snow on steep slopes, steps must be stamped in for solid footing. On hard snow, however, where the surface is solid but slippery, level steps must be made. In both cases, the steps are made by swinging the entire leg in toward the surface, not just by pushing your boot into the snow. In hard snow, you may have to use **crampons** (spiked iron plates that clamp onto your boots)—which you should have if you are a backpacker. Space your steps evenly and close together to make travel easier and to keep your balance.

When traveling *down* a snow slope, you can make use of the **plunge step** or step-by-step descending. The plunge step uses your heels a lot and can be used on **scree** (rock piles) as well as snow. On soft snow slopes, do not lean too far forward: you risk wedging your foot in a rut and suffering an injury. On hard snow, your heel will not penetrate the surface unless it has a lot of force behind it. If you do not ensure your heel enters the snow, you may slip and begin to slide.

Step-by-step descending is used when the terrain is extremely steep, the snow very deep, or you want to walk at a slower pace. You must face the slope and lower yourself step by step, thrusting the toe of each boot into the snow while maintaining an **anchor** with an ice axe.

If you are equipped with an ice axe—and you should be if you are Ranger-trained—you can rapidly descend a slope by a method known as **glissading**. For the sitting glissade, you simply sit in the snow and slide down the slope using the ice axe as a brake by digging it into the snow. You can increase your speed by lying on your back to spread body weight and lifting your feet into the air. The standing glissade is similar to skiing; position yourself as if sitting in an imaginary chair. Spread your legs outward for

This illustration demonstrates the correct position for braking yourself during a mountain fall. As you slide, roll quickly over onto your front and bury the head of the ice axe into the ground.

Climbing at an angle to a slope is easier than going straight up. The ice axe is used to give stability and to stop the climber from slipping.

balance. Put one foot slightly forward to feel for bumps and ruts. You can go faster by bringing the feet close together, reducing weight on the ice axe, and leaning forward until the boot soles are running flat along the surface like short skis. When using any form of glissading, you must bear in mind the following points:

- Only make a glissade when there is open ground in front of you.
- You must wear mittens or gloves to protect your hands and keep control of the ice axe.
- Wear heavy waterproof pants to protect your buttocks.

We have seen already how dangerous glaciers can be. So what does the U.S. Army teach about moving across them? There are several vital procedures. Take special care in areas where the glacier starts to become steeper or where it bends, as this will create dangerous features. Take care with snow bridges (which cross crevasses), as they might give way at any moment. Try to cross a glacier in the early morning when it is still cold, before ice has turned to melted water. If the glacier is covered with fresh snow, features like crevasses will be difficult to see and, therefore, climbers should be roped up to each other. It is much safer to be roped together whatever the conditions. Temperatures may be high on the glacier during the day, but climbers should take care about how much clothing they remove because, if they fall into a crevasse, the temperature will plummet. Moraines can be good routes to travel on, especially if they are made up of large blocks. However, if they consist of small rocks, pebbles, and earth, they will be loose and unstable. Be extremely careful when crossing a glacial surface stream—the bed and banks are usually hard, and smooth ice is incredibly slippery.

All mountain patrols tend to tie themselves together with ropes when moving through dangerous mountain conditions. When roped up, use about 82 feet (25 m) of rope between at least two,

Elite mountain troops practice braking their falls without the aid of an ice axe. Ice axes are generally 20–28 inches (50–70 cm) long.

and preferably three or more, people. Some rope can be coiled round the body, over the right shoulder, and under the left arm, to make a distance between walkers of about 50 feet (15 m). An overhand knot should be tied round the coils and the main rope. Loose coils of rope should never be carried, and the rope should never be slack between the climbers. If the first person falls into a crevasse, the rest of the team should quickly move backward and squat down with their heels dug into the snow to stop the fall.

Rock and steep terrain present their own challenges for the U.S. Rangers, but since their earliest days they have been trained in climbing even vertical cliffs and mountain faces. You should have a rope for tackling rock faces, but if you do not, then go down by facing the cliff on steep faces. On rock faces that are less steep, adopt a sideways position and use the hand nearest the rock face for support.

When going up, move one foot and hand at a time. Make sure you have a good hold before putting your weight on it. Avoid becoming spread-eagled. Let your legs do the work. To climb up vertical cracks in the rock face, use what the Rangers call the "chimney" technique—place your back against one surface and wedge your legs across the gap on the other. Move up slowly. Try to keep a good balance when climbing—remember it is the feet, not the hands, that should carry the weight. Above all, avoid a spread-eagled position in which you stretch too far and then cannot let go.

The following holds are used by the U.S. Army when climbing rock faces:

Push holds

Here you literally push yourself away from a rock surface while gripping the rock. This hold helps keep the climber low.

Pull holds

Used to haul yourself up. They are the easiest holds to use.

Jam holds

These involve jamming any part of the body or extremity into a crack. Place your hand into a crack and clench it into a fist, or thrust your arm into a crack and twist your elbow against one side and your hand against the other. If you are using your foot to make a jam hold, make sure you can remove it easily when you want to climb on.

Counterforce hold

This hold is made by pinching a protruding rock between the thumb and fingers and pulling outward, or by pressing inward with the arms.

Lay-back hold

Lean to one side while your hands are in a crack in the rock, then pull up with them. Your feet push against the rock—in other words, the hands and feet pull and push in opposite directions.

Mantling

Place your hands on the slab or shelf, haul yourself up, and then

Two techniques for braking yourself during an ice fall. The key is to stop before you gain momentum—victims of mountain falls have been known to achieve speeds over 60 miles per hour (96 km/h).

by straightening or locking your arms and legs, your body is raised up and you can place a leg on a higher hold.

As well as advanced climbing techniques, elite troops are also taught methods of walking. Correct walking techniques are vital to save energy. If you are not walking in snow, remember two points:

- Keep the weight of your body over your feet.
- The sole of your boot must be placed flat on the ground.

Take small steps at a steady pace. When ascending on hard ground, lock your knees with every step to rest the leg muscles. If you encounter steep slopes, remember that traversing (zig-zagging) is easier than going straight up. Turning at the end of each traverse is done by stepping off in the new direction with the uphill foot. This stops you having to cross the feet and losing your balance. Stop frequently for a rest—you make mistakes when you get tired, which can result in twisted ankles and broken legs.

For narrow stretches of uphill travel, use what is known as the **herringbone step**. This means walking with the toes pointed out. When going down, keep your back straight and knees bent, with the weight kept directly over the feet. On grassy slopes, step on the upper side of each tussock, where the ground is more level than on the lower side. When descending, it is best to traverse. Scree slopes are made up of small rocks and gravel that have collected below rock ridges and cliffs. Ascending such slopes is difficult and potentially dangerous—kick in with the toe of your upper foot to form a step. When descending, walk down the slope with your feet in a slightly pigeon-toed position using a short step. Go at a slow pace. On rocky slopes, step on top and on the uphill side of the rocks.

Walking techniques and successful navigation help U.S. Army soldiers cover the huge distances they are renowned for, and in record time. As always, safety is the key in mountain survival. Even simple injuries can be serious if the victim is on an exposed mountainside. Hence the Rangers are also experts in using ropes and harnesses to protect them from falling and slipping.

WALKING IN THE MOUNTAINS

- Conserve energy: always keep the center of gravity over your feet to make the legs do most of the work, not the arms and upper body.
- Always test holds by tapping the rock and listening for a hollow sound, which indicates instability.
- Keep hands at shoulder level to ensure blood supply to arms and hands is not reduced.
- Watch where you put your feet.
- Keep three points of contact with the rock at all times.
- Carry out slow rhythmic movements.
- Think ahead: plan moves and anticipate any difficulties.
- Keep your heels down.

ROPES AND CLIMBING

A piece of rope can be soldiers' best friend on a bleak and inhospitable mountaintop. Their knowledge of how to tie knots and use them for climbing can turn a simple rope into a lifesaver.

There are a number of specialized knots elite troops use for climbing, and the survivor should be aware of them. They are designed to make a secure anchor when tied, but be easy to untie when conditions are wet and icy.

Figure-eight loop

The figure-eight loop can be tied at the end or in the middle of a line. It gives you a fixed loop, which can be put over rocks and trees for climbing.

Manharness hitch

This is also called the butterfly knot. Follow the picture closely. It is a difficult knot to make, but it is good for tying together several people in a group so that they do not become lost in a blizzard, or for adding protection in case one of a party falls through ice or down a crevasse.

Ropes come in two varieties: walking ropes and climbing ropes. A walking rope will break with a weight of 2,000 pounds (907

Abseiling is used by elite forces as a means of entering remote or heavily protected buildings during hostage-rescue missions.

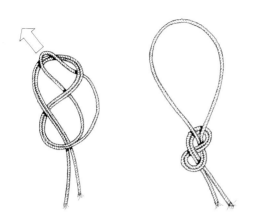

A figure-eight loop is one of the most effective climbing knots; it will not slip under pressure.

kg)—just enough to save a person on a fall, though not from a great height. A climber weighing 180 pounds (82 kg) falling 82 feet (25 m) will, when he is stopped, exert an equivalent force on the rope of 2,288 pounds (1,038 kg). That is why climbing ropes are essential. A rope intended to protect climbers against long drops should have a **breaking strain** of 4,200 pounds (1,900 kg). If a climbing rope is not available, then elite troops will improvise by tying two walking ropes together.

All mountain climbers are aware of the following dangers.

- Wet or icy rock: can make an easy route impossible.
- Snow: may cover over useful holds or hide loose rock.
- Smooth rock slabs: can be dangerous, especially if wet or icy.
- Rocks overgrown with moss or grass: treacherous when wet.
- Tufts of grass or small bushes: may be growing from loose soil that crumbles when touched.
- Rock falls: these are often caused by other climbers, heavy rain, and extreme temperature changes. In the event of a rock fall, find shelter fast, or, if this is not possible, press yourself into the slope to make yourself a small target.

Two of the U.S. Army's more advanced climbing techniques are known as **belaying** and **rappelling**. Belaying is a way of climbing up a mountainside for two or more people with ropes. One person (the climber) ascends with a rope attached around the waist. This person (known as the belayer) then ties the rope further up the slope in case the next climber falls. The belayer anchors the rope around some solid feature with a loop tied in a figure-eight, then twists the rope around the arm closest to the anchor and takes up any loose rope. The climber ties onto the rope with a knot around his waist and starts to climb. The belayer keeps the rope tight and helps the climber make the climb safely.

Rappelling is different. It helps a survivor with a rope to descend quickly by sliding down a rope that has been tied around an anchor point above him. When rappelling, ensure that the rope reaches the bottom of the drop. The anchor point should be carefully tested—

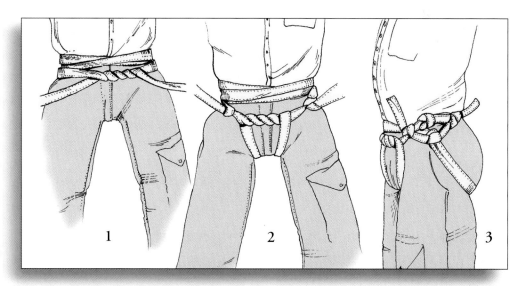

The three stages in the making of a man-harness. Always use professional climbing ropes and straps and take advice from a professional.

Israeli soldiers climb Mount Hermon in the Golan Heights region. At its peak, this mountain is 9,232 feet (2,814 m).

you must make sure that it will take your weight. Make sure too that the area is clear of loose rocks, otherwise the rope may knock them off. If this happens, they may fall on you and inflict injuries.

To rappel, the climber faces the anchor point and straddles the rope. Then he pulls it from behind, takes it around either hip, diagonally across the chest, and back over the opposite shoulder (A). From there, the rope runs to the braking hand, which is on the same side of the hip that the rope crosses. You must lean with the braking hand down and be facing slightly sideways (B). Once mastered, rappelling lets you descend quickly and safely from high mountains.

All climbers, mountain troops included, depend on what are known as anchors. Anchors are points around which a rope can be tied. They will take the weight of a climber and also be strong enough to hold him on the rope if he falls. Many natural features can be used as anchor points.

Chock stone

A **chock stone** is a stone that is securely wedged and provides an anchor point for a sling. In most cases, the rock is wedged within a crack.

Bollard

A rock **bollard** is a large rock or piece of rock over which a sling or rope can be placed in such a way that it will not slip off. You must take care to ensure that the bollard cannot be pulled loose.

Tree anchor

Trees can make very secure anchor points, though in rocky or loose soil they should be avoided if other anchor points are available.

Belaying requires the climber to anchor the rope using special pins while the second person takes the strain in case the climber falls.

Climbing walls are an excellent training tool for soldiers. This one is based at the U.S. Marine training depot on Parris Island, South Carolina.

Spike

A spike is, like its name suggests, a spiky projection of rock.

Using any of these features, and knowing how to use a rope properly, the elite soldier will be able to move around a mountain safely and securely. But sometimes you may be stuck on a mountain for a long time, which is when your other survival skills will be used.

FITNESS TRAINING

Fitness training is essential before going mountain climbing. The arms and legs will have to be strong enough to cope with holding the full body weight for hour after hour. Having insufficient strength will hamper your ability to climb.

"Fast-roping" is a method of sliding down a rope at speed. Here, a U.S. soldier is fast-roping from a Black Hawk helicopter, which can carry 11 fully equipped troops.

SHELTER AND SURVIVAL

Mountains can be very hostile places. Elite troops have learned that they must be able to find food, build a good shelter, and have the right clothing if they are to survive.

There is little food on mountains, and none at all on high cliffs. You may see some mountain goats and sheep on the lower slopes, but they are wary and difficult to approach. However, the U.S. Army surprise them by moving quietly downwind (the wind hits the animal before you) when they are feeding with their heads lowered. But remember that they are very confident climbers and you may not be—do not get injured chasing after a mountain goat, for instance. There may also be edible plants on the lower slopes. However, your first priority will be to get into the valleys, where there will be plenty of food. Water is less of a problem on high ground: melted snow, ice, and rain water can be drunk without purification.

Because mountain areas are made mostly of rock, snow, and ice, there will not be many materials available to the soldier for building shelters. It is almost always better to use your time and energy to get down from a mountain than to dig a snow hole. However, one of your party may be injured, or there may be other pressing reasons why you cannot do this.

For a snow cave to be truly effective, the walls must be one foot (30 cm) thick, although the ceiling will sink a little as the weight settles.

If you do become stranded in a mountainous region, it is very important that you get out of the wind and into some sort of shelter very quickly. The U.S. Army are experts in creating shelters using anything from branches and leaves to blocks of ice. One of the first things they teach you is to match the type of shelter you build to the terrain, natural resources available, and weather and snow conditions. Do not try to battle with nature; work in harmony with it. For example, if there are trees, you can build shelters using logs and tree trunks. If you are in the arctic away from trees, you will want to build a **snow cave** or snow trench. But whatever type of

Mountaineers shelter in a snow cave. Simply lighting a candle inside the snow cave can raise the temperature by up to 20°F (11°C).

SHELTER

The temperatures on top of a mountain can plummet many degrees below zero. When this is combined with heavy winds, the effects can be lethal in minutes unless soldiers can build a shelter to protect themselves.

shelter you choose, remember to avoid the lee side of cliffs where snow can drift and bury you, and areas where avalanches or rock falls are likely.

There are various types of shelter that can be built in mountainous conditions, and although they differ, there are common principles that you must adhere to. Do not have more than one entrance. It is unnecessary and will cause your shelter to lose heat. Try to limit the number of trips you make outside and make the trips you do make worthwhile—gather fuel and insulating material. To save yourself from going outside to the toilet, dig connecting snow caves and use one as a bathroom. Never sit or sleep on the cold snow floor; always put thick insulation under yourself (outer clothing is good for this), even if you have a sleeping bag. Shirts can be rolled up and used as pillows. Sleeping bags must be kept dry. If your bedding does get damp, turn it inside out and warm it in front of a fire. Be careful not to burn it. Keep the inside of the shelter dry by brushing all snow off clothes before entering. Any snow you do bring into the shelter will quickly turn to water so be careful. It is far better to prevent clothing from becoming damp in the first place, than to have to face the problem of drying it afterward. In harsh mountain climates, prevention is easier than than a cure.

We will now look at specific types of shelter that the U.S. Army use on survival exercises in mountain regions. With all of them, remember to watch out for snow gathering on the roof of your shelter—it may cause the roof to collapse when it gets too heavy.

A Gebirgsjäger soldier stands outside his man-made snow shelter. The Gebirgsjäger is a German mountain unit. It was formed during World War I and fought throughout World War II.

Molded dome shelter

If you have a large cloth or poncho, this shelter is one of the quickest and easiest to construct. First, build the base by piling up bark or boughs in a dome-shape and cover these with your poncho. Then cover the base with snow and wait for it to harden. When the snow has frozen in position, you can remove the poncho, bark, and twigs. You must remember to insulate the floor of the shelter with green boughs to prevent you from sleeping directly on the snow.

Snow cave

A snow cave is an underground dwelling that provides warmth and protection from freezing mountain winds. Before building your cave, first make sure the snow is deep enough to dig down into. The entrance should face downwind because the last thing you want is wind, snow, and rain blowing into your cave. Dig a small tunnel into the side of a snow drift for three feet (90 cm). Then begin to dig out from this tunnel to the right and left at right angles to the tunnel entrance. The cave should have an arched roof and be high enough to sit up inside it. If possible, make the sleeping area higher than the tunnel entrance. Because hot air rises, this will be the warmest part of the shelter. The roof should be at least an inch and a quarter (3 cm) thick and the entrance should be blocked up with a backpack, poncho, or snow block to retain warmth.

The cave should have at least two ventilation holes: one in the roof and one in the door that lets air in and out. Poisonous gases can be released when cooking food so it is essential these have a means of escape.

Trench shelter

If you are stranded in a snow storm and need to find shelter quickly, the trench shelter provides basic and temporary protection. Find a large drift of snow and cut it into blocks. Dig a trench about one foot (30 cm) deep and the same wide. It should be as long as you are tall. Then use the snow slabs to build a wall around the trench. Make a roof with large slabs. Make sure that you create at least one ventilation hole. The trench shelter should only be temporary. When the storm passes, build an igloo.

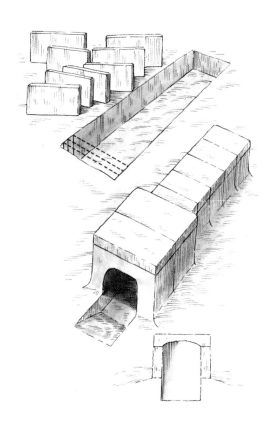

A snow trench can protect soldiers from the effects of wind-chill.

Lean-to shelter

As well as being easy to construct, the principle benefit of this shelter is that it can be used all-year round. It provides shade, protects you from rain and snow, and keeps you warm. Cut some equal-sized branches and tie them together in a grid pattern. When complete, lean the structure between two trees and tie the top of the grid to the tree trunks. Once you have the framework in place, cover it with leaves and other foliage. If you are feeling confident, you can turn the lean-to into an A-frame shelter by building another lean-to and leaning it on the other side of the tree trunks. Do not forget to insulate the floor.

Although the roof and sides of your shelter will keep you warm and dry, you will not get the most from it unless you insulate the floor. Spruce or pine boughs give the most comfortable, dry sleeping area. Stones can be heated by the fire and then placed inside the shelter to provide even more heat. Above all, try to keep your camp neat, tidy, and dry; you do not want to have to venture far from your shelter.

Always ensure that you have plenty of fuel supplies for your fire. Decide early on what type of fire you want. For example, if you

When making camp, it is important to place the fire away from coniferous trees. A forest fire can move at speeds of over 30 miles per hour (48 km/h) if it is pushed by strong winds.

build a log fire, you will have lots of warmth and light. However, it will burn quickly and therefore requires lots of fuel. In a snow area, you could use up a lot of energy by having to gather more wood. Choose a fire that burns for a long time and requires the minimum attention. The most important thing is that you do not let your fire go out.

Insects can be a problem in snow and ice areas, especially in summer. You may not even consider them when you are selecting a shelter site, but you should: they can make your life very hard. As a general rule, the U.S. Army stay away from deep woods. This is where many insects live and are in their greatest numbers. Build your shelter where there is plenty of sunlight and breeze—there will not be as many insects. If you are really being pestered by them (and insects can make the survivor's life hell), make a fire or a number of fires and ensure there is always some smoke around you. You may not like it very much, but the insects will like it a lot less. Use small fires with green or rotten damp wood to guarantee plenty of insect-repelling smoke.

Of course, fire not only has the advantage of repelling insects; it will also keep you warm. If you do have to make a shelter on a mountain, be sure to also build a fire. Use any material that is available—sticks, grasses, even dried goat manure if you can find it. Basically, use anything that will burn.

Of course, the most important source of warmth is the clothing that you wear. The U.S. Army have special uniforms designed to cope with everything the mountains can throw at them. Depending on how high you are up a mountain, you will either be cold or very cold. Having the right kind of clothing will make a big difference.

The most important principle for mountain clothing is what is known as the **layering system**. This means wearing many layers of clothing—each layer traps in air, which is warmed up by the body. Whereas climbers of 50 or 100 years ago had only basic clothing, today you can buy modern materials that are superb at keeping in heat while repelling the snow, rain, and wind found on mountaintops.

The first layer is known as the base layer. This is usually a thin layer of synthetic material. Its purpose is to transfer sweat from the

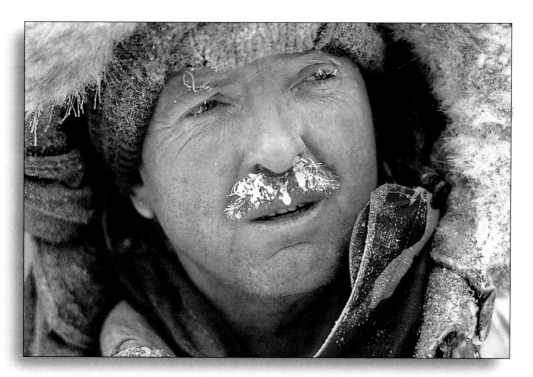

The head is the most important part of the body to protect in sub-zero conditions. This U.S. Ranger's woolen hat is a wise choice because wool continues to warm the body even when wet.

Crampons are an essential piece of kit for any climber working in icy environments. The sharp metal spikes at the front can be dug straight into the slipperiest ice for a secure foothold.

skin away from the body, while being too thin to absorb water that may be coming in from outside—this is known as "breathable" material. The result is that you should always remain reasonably dry despite the level of exertion or outside conditions.

Next comes the insulating layer. The latest and most effective insulating material is fleece. If you are going to buy a fleece, it is worth taking care to choose the right one. There are different thicknesses and some have "breathable" material inserted. There are other factors to consider, such as ventilation zippers and stretch fleeces. Finally, there is the outer layer, also known as the "shell" layer. Ideally, this should be a breathable fabric jacket that has elasticized wrists and waistband, and a large hood to protect your face from the biting mountain winds.

Make sure that you keep all your clothing clean. If it gets dirty and wet, it will not work as well at keeping you warm. Therefore you should clean off any mud at the end of each day in the mountains.

Boots are important for any soldier, but for troops destined for the mountains they are vital. There is a huge variety of boots available on the market, most of which are good. However, it is important to remember that boots are built in different ways to suit different jobs. Before buying, talk to an expert in a reputable, outdoor equipment shop (but always bear in mind that the salesperson's job is to sell you something). Do your own research through magazines, which sometimes tell you the best type of boots for your purpose.

The major types of conditions for which you will require different boots are hillwalking, winter mountaineering, and snow- and ice-climbing. Flexible boots are good for hillwalking. But for mountain survival use, wear boots with very stiff soles and supportive uppers (the part of the boot that covers the top of your foot). Crampons can be added when necessary (metal spikes that can be used for extra grip on ice), and will be more effective on this kind of boot.

Soldiers complete their mountain equipment with three essential pieces of kit: helmet, ice axe, and ski stick. Helmets are vital to protect the head not only from falls but also from rocks dropping onto your head from above you. Again, find an expert who can tell you about the good helmets, and then buy the best one that you can afford. An important point to remember is that once your helmet has taken a heavy knock, you should replace it because it might be weakened. Ice axes are a vital piece of safety equipment, and elite soldiers will also keep theirs ready tucked into their belts.

Ice axes can be used for many things. The long handle can be used to test how deep snow is, and can also be used as a support when climbing up steep slopes. If soldiers slip and start to slide down the mountainside, they are trained quickly to use their ice axes as brakes by digging it into the ice and hanging on. Another good item of safety equipment carried by U.S. Army mountain troops is a ski stick. This will make movement through snow easier by acting as a walking stick. It can also help you to walk further by taking some of the pressure off your legs.

However much equipment soldiers carry, they always have to be prepared for the unexpected. As the next chapter will tell us, the mountains are full of dangers, and it takes the expert advice of the elite forces to guide us out of trouble.

RECOVERING FROM A FALL

If a Ranger slips on the ice, he rolls over with his ice axe and digs the point into the ground. If he hangs on, then he should come to a complete stop within a few yards. If the soldier does not have an ice axe, he should dig the point of his shoes into the ice and use his hands to find holds in the snow.

This soldier wears typical arctic combat clothing. He avoids cotton clothes or under garments since wet cotton releases body heat 240 times faster than when it is dry.

DANGERS

From avalanches to rock falls, the U.S. Army soldier is always on the lookout for danger in the mountains. Quick responses and good techniques are needed to save lives in split-second disasters.

The sheer unpredictability of weather conditions on mountains can pose a number of hazards. The weather can change quickly from pleasant sunshine to gloomy skies and driving rain or snow storms. Mountains attract long periods of harsh weather. The wind blows most strongly on mountain tops and across ridges because wind speed increases with height. Do not underestimate a strong wind or its chilling effect—it will drain your energy and heat as you try to stay balanced while being buffeted. Also remember that rain tends to be more frequent and heavier in the mountains. It can soak you to the skin in a short space of time and make you dangerously cold —so try to keep as dry as possible. In addition, you will not be able to see as far due to low cloud, driving rain, mist, **whiteouts** (where the snow swirls about you so you cannot see), or storms.

Another danger that elite troops have to be aware of is lightning. This is very common in mountains. It is attracted to summits and pinnacles. In a thunderstorm avoid summits, exposed ridges, pinnacles, gullies containing water, and lone trees. Leave wet ropes and metal equipment at least 50 feet (15 m) from your shelter if

Camouflage clothing is good when hunting. The U.S. Army has its own unique camouflage pattern called ASAT (All Seasons All Terrains).

possible. Avoid vertical cliffs: they are excellent conductors of electricity. Put yourself in a sitting position with the knees drawn up against the chest. This is the best protection against the electricity flowing through the earth.

Remember, mountain troops always get information about the weather before they set off into the mountains, and you should do the same. Listen to the weather forecasts, or better still, ring the local meteorological office for a personal weather service. It is very important to give the exact area and time required for the forecast. You should ask for information about the valley and mountain top weather, temperatures, winds, rain and snowfall, visibility, likelihood of a freeze, and any rapid changes approaching.

Lightning is a danger in the mountains. Its powerful electric current generates 50,000°F (27,500°C) of heat through a single bolt.

Some mountainous areas are susceptible to avalanches. The Alpine mountains in Switzerland have up to 10,000 avalanches each year.

Obviously, you will be unable to do this if you are a survivor, but there is really no excuse for the backpacker to be caught unawares.

One of the biggest, and most spectacular dangers, is that of the avalanche. Avalanches happen when tons of snow suddenly run down a mountainside. They can travel at over 100 miles per hour (160 km/h), and anybody caught in their path can be carried hundreds of yards before being buried in tons of snow. Avalanches can occur wherever there is snow. Yet certain conditions make them more likely. If the snow is well bound together, then there is less a risk of avalanche. If there are differences in the hardness of layers of snow, then the risk of avalanche increases.

You can assess the possibility of an avalanche happening by digging into the snow. If you notice that the snow is a mixture of hard and soft snow on top of one another, this is quite a good sign that an avalanche could happen there. Water is a lubricant, so if the snow is very wet, it will be denser and heavier, and more likely to slide. A rough guide to the wetness of snow is that if you can make a snowball out of the snow, it is quite wet. If your gloves are dripping wet from handling the snow, it is very wet.

There are several other signs a Ranger looks for to assess the possibility of avalanches. If the ground is hard and smooth, then snow is more likely to slide over it. Long grass will also provide a slippery surface for snow. If a slope is convex—meaning it bulges outward—it is more likely to have an avalanche. Also, the steeper the slope, the more likely the snow is to slide off it.

The most common type of avalanche is called wind slab, and is caused by the effect of wind on falling or fallen snow. Wind slab snow is chalky in appearance, has a fine texture, and makes a squeaky noise when walked on. Avalanches can also be caused when powdery snow accumulates in conditions of no or little wind. Over 16 inches (40 cm) of fresh snow is an indicator of a high risk of this kind of avalanche.

LIGHTNING STRIKES

If you are on a mountaintop and you feel your hair and neck tingling and crackling, lightning could be about to strike. Throw yourself to the ground immediately to protect yourself.

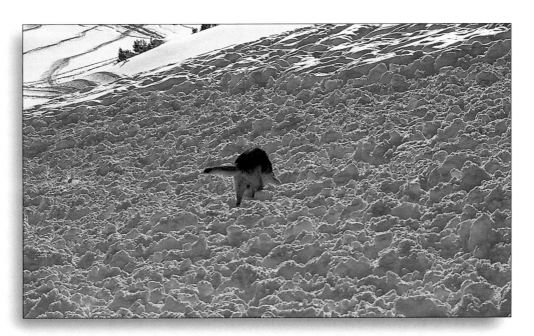

A dog searches for survivors in the snow. Dogs are used for search and rescue missions because their sense of smell is up to 200 times better than that of a human and their hearing is 150 percent better.

The U.S. Army give the following advice for crossing avalanche danger areas. Cross a danger zone one at a time, connected by a rope. Cross the slope as high up as possible. Take advantage of any protection, such as rock outcrops. Yet however careful you are, avalanches will sometimes happen on their own. As they operate in mountainous terrain, all mountain soldiers must have an in-depth knowledge of the warning signs.

- Avalanches usually occur in the same area. After a path has been smoothed, it is easier for another slide to occur. Steep, open gullies, pushed-over trees, and tumbled rocks are signs of slide slopes.
- Snowballs tumbling downhill or sliding snow is an indication of an avalanche area.

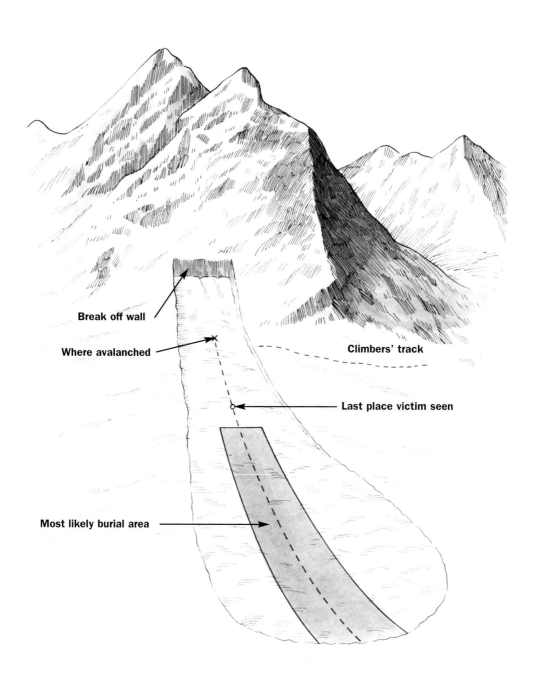

Break off wall

Where avalanched

Climbers' track

Last place victim seen

Most likely burial area

This diagram explains how to search for someone buried in an avalanche. The most dangerous type of avalanche is one made of wet snow, because it solidifies when it stops moving.

- If snow sounds hollow, there is danger of an avalanche.
- If snow cracks, and cracks persist or run, a slab avalanche is imminent.

If the avalanche does begin, and you are caught in it, the U.S. Army give this advice. Remove your backpack and skis and try to run toward the side of an avalanche. Sometimes you can "swim" in an avalanche. If swimming movements are possible, a double-action back stroke is the most effective, with your back to the force of the avalanche and the head up. Keep your mouth shut. In a powder snow avalanche, cover your mouth and nose with clothing to form an air space. Save your strength for when the avalanche loses

A helicopter in a snow storm. The helicopter is a Bell UH-1 Iroquois, which is used by the armies of more than 60 countries worldwide.

momentum and settles. You must try to get to an air space near the surface, otherwise your chances of survival are minimal. Try to dig slowly to the surface and do not panic. Conserve oxygen by not shouting, which is unlikely to be heard anyway.

Rangers are also trained in techniques for rescuing a team mate who has been caught in an avalanche. If you see someone taken by an avalanche, first mark the spot where you saw him or her before the avalanche fell, and then the place where the avalanche hit the person. Continue in a straight line beneath these two points to find the most likely place the person was buried. Then call for help, but do not leave the area to find assistance that is more than 15 minutes away—the victim might suffocate in that time. Look for anything like personal items that may show where the burial site is. Check the area by probing with an axe shaft or ski stick. If you find the victim, clear the mouth and nose of snow to help the person breathe. Remove the weight of snow from his chest.

Following the advice of mountain troops should help you to avoid or survive and avalanche. Another emergency the U.S. Army are prepared for is if someone falls down a crevasse. Do not go too close to the edge to look down—you could end up joining the

AVALANCHES

Remember that you can not outrun an avalanche. The force and speed of an avalanche can tear down trees, so try to get out of the way quickly by moving to the side.

person down the crevasse. Pass a rope down with a loop in it. The person in the crevasse can put a foot in it and you can then haul them up. It usually takes three strong people to haul an unconscious person out of a crevasse. But remember, speed is vital —temperatures in crevasses are absolutely freezing.

Though all these procedures can help save lives, mountains are still places where injuries can easily occur. Our next chapter will look at the most common first-aid situations that elite troops face in the mountains.

If you fall through an ice hole your limbs will start to freeze in just four minutes, you will pass out in about seven minutes, and be dead in about 15 minutes.

FIRST AID

In wartime, the U.S. Army are used to tending injured people. But even in peacetime, first-aid skills are essential to help those injured on the mountains.

Many accidents can happen on the mountainside. You can get hit by a rockfall, burned in a camp fire, or suffer friction burns if ropes slip quickly through your hands. Yet the commonest first-aid situations are those involving broken bones and **altitude sickness**. We will see what altitude sickness is in a moment, but first we shall look at how the U.S. Army deals with people with broken bones.

It is not always obvious when someone has a broken bone. Usually a broken limb has severe black and blue bruising, and sometimes it has been knocked out of shape in an unnatural place. If you are not sure whether it is broken, treat it as if it is. Remember that the following procedures are intended only to help protect the injured limb until you can get the person to hospital or medical attention.

Firstly, stop casualties from moving around (preferably get them to lie down) and keep the injured area still. If the injured limb is bleeding, press hard over the wound with a clean pad until the bleeding is stopped. Next comes the most difficult part of the first-

This type of stretcher is called a "scoop stretcher." It is designed to lift the injured person in the position in which they were found.

aid procedure. When, say, someone's forearm is broken, the bone may be broken into two or more pieces. This often means that the bone is no longer straight, but is crooked because of the breaks. Your objectives should be to put all these pieces of bone into a straight line through a process of called **traction**. Traction is done by pulling a broken limb straight and then relaxing it back into the normal position. This helps protect the broken limb from further damage and lets the blood flow normally around the limb. Please remember: this would not usually be done in a situation where rescue services are only minutes away. Only do it in a survival situation when you are days away from rescue, and it is only suitable for broken arms or legs.

Traction is performed by gently but firmly pulling on the broken limb. Do this first in the direction the bone is pointing, then swing

The recovery position promotes easy breathing and also ensures that potentially dangerous fluid build-up drains out of the mouth.

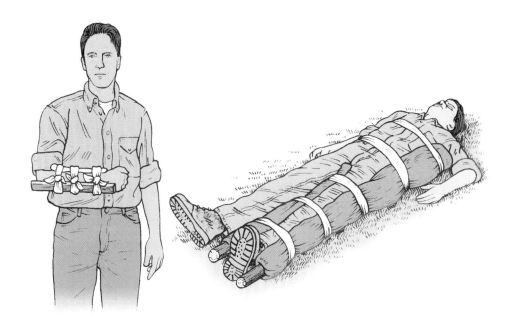

Splinting broken limbs protects them from further damage. The splinting method on the right should be used when transporting an injured person long distances.

it back in line with the original limb position. The U.S. Army recommend that you do this slowly over a period of 10 to 15 minutes. Try to get the injured person to relax while you are doing this, as it will make your job easier. Once the limb is fully extended, make it straight as it should be normally—you can get someone else to do this for maximum accuracy—and then relax your pull.

Once you have done this, your second priority is to keep the injured limb still through a technique known as **splinting**. Splints can be made on the spot in a survival situation. Splints require three main materials. First find something rigid, like a ski, ice-axe handle, or straight branch. This is called a stabilizer. Even flexible materials such as towels, magazines, and coats can be rolled up and used as stabilizers. Secondly, you need string, tape, bandage, or rope to tie the stabilizer securely to the broken limb. Thirdly, you need some kind of material padding to keep the break comfortable and fixed in place.

Rangers follow a standard procedure when binding a broken limb.

- Only splint a limb that has been straightened by traction.
- Bind the stabilizer (or two stabilizers, one on either side if you need it) to the broken limb. Make sure that the joints either side of the break cannot move. For example, if the forearm is broken, the splint should also hold the elbow and the wrist. This is done by running a padded stabilizer down the length of the limb and tying it in place with the bandages. Be careful you do not tie too tight. Check the color of the skin and nails in the hands or feet. If it is going white or blue, then you have tied too tight, and you should relax the knots a bit until the color is normal.

There are many exceptions to this procedure depending on what part of the body is injured. All U.S. Army soldiers undergo extensive first-aid training, and so should you before you practice any medical treatment in a survival situation.

Sprains, strains, and bruises are everyday hazards in mountain environments (and everywhere else—almost all of us know what a twisted ankle feels like). Though they are not serious in themselves, they can be dangerous because they can leave a person stuck on a freezing mountainside. Mountain troops learn a standard technique to treat these, commonly known as the RICE procedure.

Rest the injured part
Ice—chill the wound with an ice pack or cold compress
Compress the injury
Elevate the injured part

This procedure can reduce the swelling and pain that are usually a part of these types of injuries. We will illustrate the procedure by referring to a sprained ankle, but the same could be used for any limb or bruised area of the body.

Mountain climbing is a surprisingly safe sport. Out of 60,000 American mountain climbers in 1999, only 30 were killed in accidents.

STAYING WARM

The cold can kill. Watch out for anyone who is shivering violently and having trouble thinking or talking. They could be getting dangerously cold, so try to warm them up as quickly as possible.

First, get the casualty to lie down. Then take the twisted ankle and lift it higher than the rest of the body. This stops blood filling up the ankle and making it swell so much. Fill a piece of material with something cold—snow or a piece of ice are good. Press this directly over the injury for about 10 to 15 minutes. Then wrap the ankle in a elasticized bandage or some other bandage that gives lots of support. This compression will also help reduce swelling, but check it is not too tight and release it briefly every hour to help circulation. Then keep the ankle raised in this position. Once the swelling has stopped, after about 24 hours, start soaking the ankle in warm water two or three times a day, as warmth will aid the healing process. With a bad sprain or strain, the ankle or any other limb can be splinted to provide some extra healing support. Broken limbs and sprained joints can happen anywhere, and the soldier is always prepared to deliver first aid.

An illness that occurs almost only on mountaintops is something called altitude sickness. This is very serious—it can kill even strong, healthy people like mountain troops. It is caused by the lack of oxygen in the air at high altitudes above 8,000 feet (2,400 m). Human beings need plenty of oxygen in their blood to survive, and we get this when we breathe. At high altitude, less oxygen goes into the blood and the person can become very ill.

If troops are going to very high altitudes, they will do it slowly and in stages to get used to the changes in the air. It usually takes about two to five days to get used to a high altitude. Soldiers might also take oxygen cylinders with them. They can use these to breathe with if the symptoms of altitude sickness appear. Leave extra time for a journey through high-altitude environments because you will become quickly exhausted by the lack of air.

There are two different types of altitude sickness, but all elite soldiers will know the symptoms to look out for. These are:

Altitude makes soldiers very tired and can affect their ability to remember facts and orders. Rest and plenty of water is essential.

Type 1
- Headache and feeling sick. Tiredness. Sleepiness. Dizziness.
- More acute head pain. Vomiting.
- The person starts staggering and becomes confused.
- Unconsciousness.

Type 2
- Harsh coughing.
- Difficult breathing.
- Severe problems with breathing.
- Unconsciousness and the breathing stops.

In both cases, quick action is needed. Naturally, the fact that both conditions are caused by high altitude means that you should get the patient to a lower altitude. Be careful—the person is weak, so do not rush them or they may become more ill. Traveling only 1,640 feet (550 m) downhill can start to make the person feel better. But ideally you should descend about 2,000–4,000 feet (660–1,320 m) for the best results. When you are at a safe altitude, give the person plenty of rest and get them to professional medical help straight away.

The soldiers of the U.S. Rangers and 10th Mountain Division are experts at mountain first aid, but the biggest lesson they teach is not to get injured or ill in the first place. They are some of the world's toughest soldiers, but they have lots of respect for the mountains. They are extremely dangerous places and can beat even the strongest soldier.

A paramedic talks to an injured climber. Talking to injured people is vital to reassure them and help them retain consciousness. Hearing is the last sense to fail, even before death, so talking always helps.

GLOSSARY

Achnacarry Commando School A Scottish training center for the U.S. Rangers during World War II.

Altitude sickness An illness brought on by having to adjust the body to very high altitudes, such as is found on mountaintops.

American Civil War A war that took place in 1861–65 between the United States, known as the "Union," and 11 Southern states, known as the "Confederacy."

Anchor In mountaineering, an anchor is something that can hold your weight when you tie a rope to it.

Avalanche A powerful wave of snow and ice, which runs down a mountainside at great speed.

Belaying A way of climbing up a mountainside for two or more people with ropes.

Bollard A large rock or piece of rock over which a sling or rope can be placed in such a way that it will not slip off.

Breaking strain The maximum weight a piece of rope can take before it snaps.

Chock stone A stone that is securely wedged and provides an anchor point for a sling.

Crampons Spiked iron plates that clamp onto your boots to stop you slipping when walking on ice.

Crevasses Cracks in a glacier, through which a mountaineer can fall.

D-Day The invasion of German-occupied France in World War II by the Allies on June 6, 1944.

Glacier A river of ice that flows at a speed that depends largely on its size and the slope on which it travels.

Glissading A way of traveling down a mountain by sliding on the snow but controlling the speed with a ice axe.

Gradient The steepness with which a mountain goes up or down.

Herringbone step Walking with the toes pointed out when going uphill for extra grip.

Ice axe A sharp tool with two pick heads and a long handle, for use in snow and ice.

Layering system Wearing many layers of clothing—each layer traps in air, which is warmed up by the body.

Moraine Crushed rock picked up by a glacier as it slowly travels through mountains and valleys.

Pearl Harbor The harbor of the U.S. fleet, which was bombed by the Japanese on December 7, 1941.

Plunge step A way to walk on snow that uses the heels to create a solid foothold.

Ranger Training Center One of the first places for Ranger training at Fort Benning, Georgia.

Rappelling Descending quickly by sliding down a rope that has been tied around an anchor point above you.

Revolutionary War 1775–1783. A war that was fought between 13 British colonies and Britain itself. The war ended with the British defeated and the United States being born.

Scree Lots of small stones that cover the side of a mountain.

Snow cave A shelter made by digging straight into a snow drift.

Splinting Keeping a broken limb stable by tying it to a rigid support.

Timberline The area on a mountain where few trees grow at all because of the high altitude.

Traction In first aid, traction means steadily pulling a broken limb back into its original shape.

Traversing Going up a mountain in a zigzag pattern to make walking easier.

Vietnam War A war in Southeast Asia, in which the United States fought between 1965 and 1973.

Washington, George Commander of the Continental Army during the Revolutionary War, and the first president of the United States.

Whiteouts Storms in which the snow fills the air so that you cannot see.

EQUIPMENT REQUIREMENTS

Headwear
Safety helmet
Woolen, face-covering helmet
Woolen/thermal hat
Face protector

Clothing
Waterproof/windproof outer jacket
Thermal underjacket/fleece
Waterproof pants
Thermal underclothes
Spare socks
Snow goggles

Footwear
Walking boots
Gaiters
Spare laces
Crampons
Skis
Snowshoes
Climbing boots (different boots are
    needed for different environ-
    ments, so check before you go)

Load-carrying equipment
Backpack
Small carry sack
(All must be waterproof)

Survival equipment
Climbing rope
Walking rope

Carabiners (metal clips to which
    ropes can be attached)
Climbing anchors
Ice axe
Medical pack
Mess pack and knife/fork/spoon
Water bottle and mug
Survival knife
Lockable/retractable knife
Tent
Climbing and walking ropes
Sleeping bag
Plastic sheeting (to build
    shelters/make solar stills)
Sleeping mat
Survival bag
Telescopic walking stick or ski stick
Shovel/spade (foldable)
Compass
Watch
Chronograph
Flares
Signaling mirror (heliograph)
Binoculars
Map case
Wash pack
Matches
Flint and steel firelighter
Snare wire
Water purification tablets
Whistle
Candle (some candles are made to
    be edible)

CHRONOLOGY

June 1944	2000 men are picked for Rangers training. The 500 that survive are called 1st Ranger Battalion.
July 13, 1943	10th Light Division (Alpine) is created.
June 6, 1944	U.S. Army Rangers are some of the first ashore in the D-Day landings.
November 6, 1944	10th Light Division (Alpine) is renamed the 10th Mountain Division.
January 28, 1945	The 10th Mountain Division goes into action in the mountains of Italy against the Germans.
August 1945	The Japanese surrender and World War II ends.
1950–51	The U.S. Rangers fight in the Korean War.
June 15, 1954	The 10th Mountain Division becomes the 10th Infantry Division.
June 14, 1958	The 10th Mountain Division is disbanded.
1965–1973	Ranger soldiers take part in the Vietnam War.
1983	The U.S. Army Rangers fight during the U.S. invasion of the island of Grenada.
February 13, 1985	The 10th Mountain Division is reformed.
1990–1991	Soldiers of the 10th Mountain Division and U.S. Rangers serve in the Gulf War.
1992–1994	10th Mountain Division soldiers go on humanitarian operations in Somalia, Africa.
October 3–4, 1993	U.S. Rangers and 10th Mountain Division soldiers fight a heavy battle in Mogadishu, Somalia.
1994–1995	10th Mountain Division soldiers take part in Operation Restore Democracy in Haiti.
1997–1999	Soldiers of the 10th Mountain Division conduct peacekeeping operations in Bosnia, Yugoslavia.
2001	Both units return to America after security force (SFOR) operations in Bosnia.
September 11, 2001	In response to terrorist attacks in America, U.S. military, including the U.S. Rangers and Army Mountain Division, are put on the highest level of military alert since the Cuban Missile Crisis.

RECRUITMENT INFORMATION

U.S. Rangers

To join the U.S. Rangers, recruits must first be U.S. citizens, have no criminal record or history of drug use, and have a high school diploma. After passing U.S. Army Basic Training, they must undergo the Ranger Orientation Program (ROP). Recruits must gain an 80 percent pass rate in all Army Physical Fitness Test (APFT) events:

• Six chin-ups with palms facing you
• Five-mile (8-km) run in under 40 minutes
• 250-feet (75-m) swim wearing boots, uniform, and weapon
• 12-mile (19 km) road march with weapon and 45 pounds (17 kg) rucksack in   three hours

In addition, the recruit must perform well in psychological tests and interviews, and score 70 percent in an exam about Ranger history.

To find out more about the U.S. Rangers, visit the following websites:
http://www.ranger.org
http://www.military-sites-online.com
http://www.75rangers.org
http://www.specialoperations.com
http://www.rangerring.com

10th Mountain Division

To join the 10th Mountain Division, recruits must first be U.S. citizens, have no criminal record or history of drug use, and have a high school diploma. Then they must pass the U.S. Army Basic Training Program.

To find out more about the 10th Mountain Division, visit the following websites:
http://www.10thmtndivassoc.org
http://www.dtic.mil
http://www.biathlon.net/10th_mtn.html
http://www.drum.army.mil
http://gowest.coalliance.org/exhib/gallery1/battle.htm

FURTHER READING

Cinnamon, Jerry. *The Complete Climbers Handbook*. New York: McGraw-Hill Professional Publishing, 2000.

Darman, Peter. *The Survival Handbook*. Mechanisburg, Pa.: Stackpole, 1998.

Dusenbery, Harris. *North Apennines and Beyond with the 10th Mountain Division*. Portland, Ore.: Binford & Mort Publishing, 2001.

Isaac, Jeffrey. *The Outward Bound Wilderness First-Aid Handbook*. New York: The Lyons Press, 1998.

Katz, Samuel. *America's Mountain Soldiers: The 10th Mountain Division*. Coralridge, Pa.: Marco Polo Import Inc., 1995.

Kurtz, Henry. *US Army*. Topeka, Kan.: Econo-Clad Books, 1999.

Landau, Alan and Frieda Landau. *Airborne Rangers* (Power Series). Osceola, Wis.: Motorbooks International, 1992.

Luebben, Craig. *How to Ice Climb* (How to Rock Climb Series). Helena, Mon.: Falcon Publishing Company, 1999.

McNab, Chris. *First Aid Survival Manual*. Edison, N.J.: Chartwell, 2001.

Raleigh, Duane and John Long. *Clip and Go* (How to Rock Climb Series). Helena, Mon.: Falcon Publishing Company, 1998.

Rottman, Gordon. *Inside the US Army*. Mechanisburg, Pa.: Stackpole Books, 1998.

ABOUT THE AUTHOR

Dr. Chris McNab has written and edited numerous books on military history and elite forces survival. His publications to date include *German Paratroopers of World War II, The Illustrated History of the Vietnam War, First Aid Survival Manual,* and *Special Forces Endurance Techniques,* as well as many articles and features in other works. Forthcoming publications include books on the SAS, while Chris's wider research interests lie in literature and ancient history. Chris lives in South Wales, U.K.

INDEX

References in italics refer to illustrations